The GARFIELD Gallery

Jim Davis

HODDER AND STOUGHTON
LONDON SYDNEY AUCKLAND TORONTO

GARFIELD DESIGNS

The forty-eight GARFIELD illustrations within this book have been reproduced from posters by kind permission of the manufacturers:

Argus Communications

Argus Communications distribute a wide range of GARFIELD merchandise which includes:

Posters · Greeting Cards · Postcards
Stationery · Calendars · Diaries
Giftwrap & Tags · Clothing · Badges
Fun Accessories · Stickers

These products are available from most leading greeting card shops, stationers and department stores. For further information why not contact Argus direct at:
Customer Enquiries
Argus Communications, DLM House,
Edinburgh Way, Harlow, Essex CM20 2HL
Tel (0279) 39441

British Library Cataloguing in Publication Data

Davis, Jim
the Garfield Gallery
I. Title
741.5'973   NC1429

ISBN 0-340-33059-7 (paperback)
ISBN 0-340-35767-3 (cased)

Garfield Comic Strips: Copyright © 1981, 1982, 1983
United Feature Syndicate, Inc.

Copyright © 1983 United Feature Syndicate, Inc.
First published in Great Britain 1983 (paperback)
Third impression 1984
First published in Great Britain 1984 (cased)

Published by Hodder and Stoughton Children's Books, a division of Hodder and Stoughton Ltd, Mill Road, Dunton Green, Sevenoaks, Kent TN13 2YJ.

Printed in Spain by Artes Gráficas Toledo, S.A.
D. L. TO: 769 -1984

IT'S NICE TO BE LIKED
JUST THE WAY YOU ARE

JIM DAVIS

1-24

© 1982 United Feature Syndicate, Inc.

NEVER TRUST A SMILING CAT

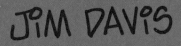

YOU KNOW, YOU'RE A VERY LUCKY CAT, GARFIELD

YOU HAVE JUST ABOUT EVERYTHING A CAT COULD WANT

YOU HAVE YOUR SANCTUM SANCTORUM

MY HIDEY-HOLE

YOU HAVE YOUR TEDDY BEAR

MY CONFIDANT

YOU HAVE YOUR DOG

MY SCRATCHING POST

JIM DAVIS

2-14

AND YOU HAVE ME, YOUR LOVING COMPANION

MY FOOD-FIXER AND LITTER BOX CHANGER

© 1981 United Feature Syndicate, Inc.

1-4

JIM DAVIS

Welcome to the Funny Farm

JIM DAVIS

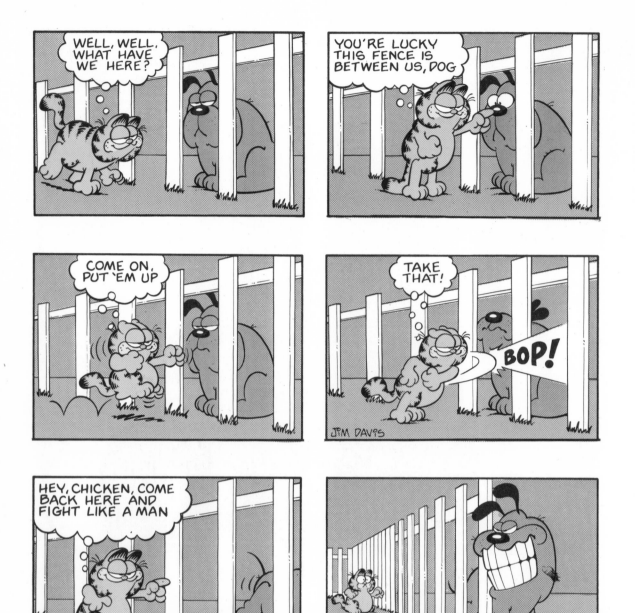

© 1983 United Feature Syndicate, Inc.   3-6

For every action there is an equal and opposite reaction

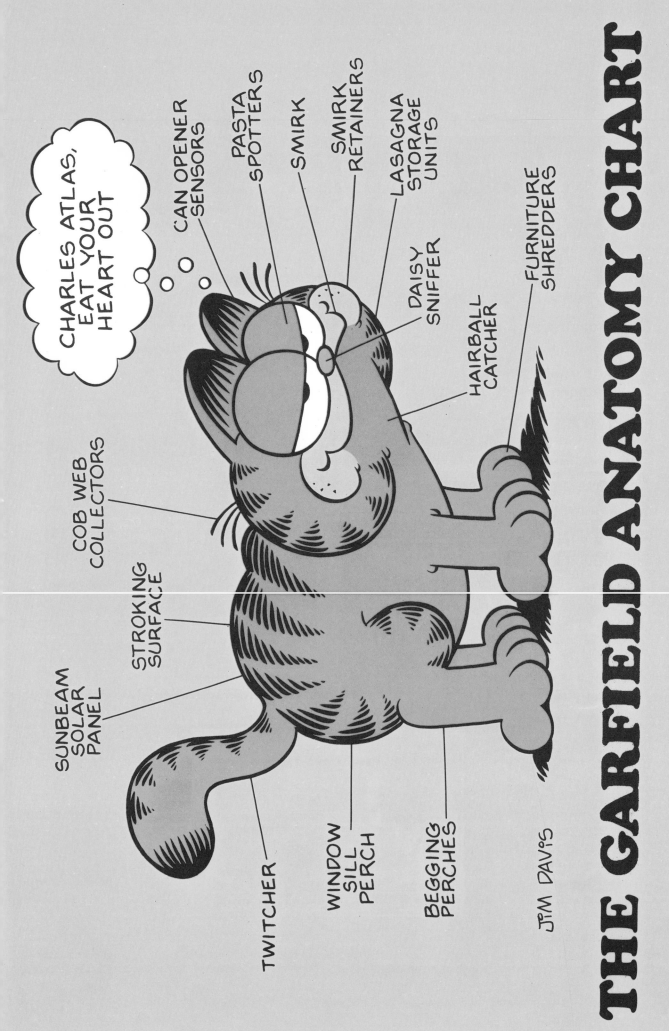

STUDYING IS MORE FUN WITH A GOOD FRIEND

JIM DAVIS

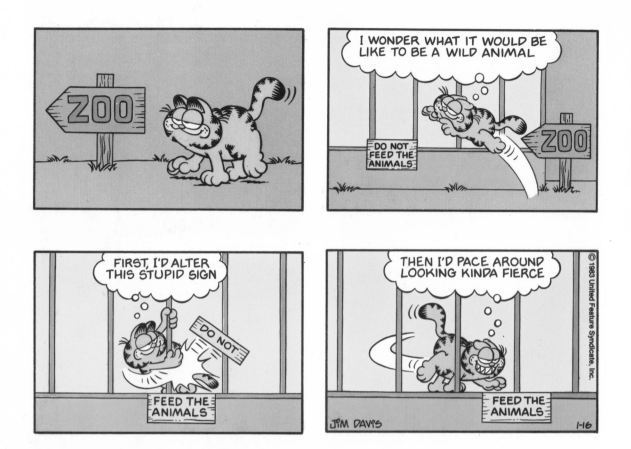

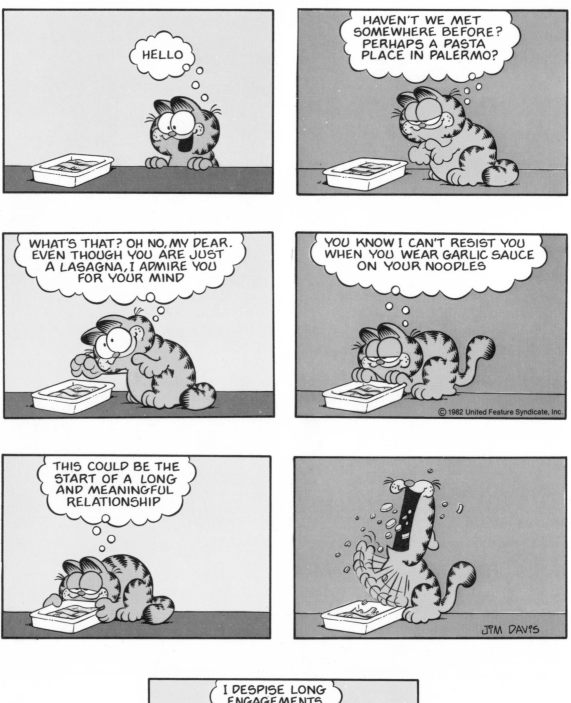

An active imagination is a wonderful thing

You know it's Monday when your down vest meets up with its former owner

JIM DAVIS

ONCE MY EATING GAINS MOMENTUM, IT'S HARD TO SLOW DOWN

JIM DAVIS

IF YOU CAN'T CONVINCE'M... CONFUSE'M

JIM DAVIS